The Library of the Middle Ages™

Richard the Lionheart and the Third Crusade

The English King Confronts Saladin, AD 1191

David Hilliam

rosen
central™

The Rosen Publishing Group, Inc., New York

Published in 2004 by The Rosen Publishing Group, Inc.
29 East 21st Street, New York, NY 10010

First Edition

Library of Congress Cataloging-in-Publication Data

Hilliam, David.
Richard the Lionheart and the Third Crusade: the English king confronts Saladin, AD 1191/David Hilliam.—1st ed.
   p. cm.—(The library of the Middle Ages)
Summary: Relates how King Richard I of England and his troops nearly wrested Jerusalem from Muslim leader Saladin and the Saracens during the Third Crusade in 1191 AD.
Includes bibliographical references and index.
ISBN 0-8239-4213-9 (library binding)
1. Richard I, King of England, 1157–1199—Juvenile literature.
2. Crusades—Third, 1189–1192—Juvenile literature. 3. Saladin, Sultan of Egypt and Syria, 1137–1193—Juvenile literature. [1. Richard I, King of England, 1157–1199. 2. Saladin, Sultan of Egypt and Syria, 1137–1193. 3. Crusades—Third, 1189–1192. 4. Kings, queens, rulers, etc. 5. Christianity—Relations—Islam—History—To 1500. 6. Islam—Relations—Christianity—History—To 1500.]
I. Title. II. Series.
DA207.H55 2003
956'.014—dc21
                                                    2002156674

Manufactured in the United States of America

Table of Contents

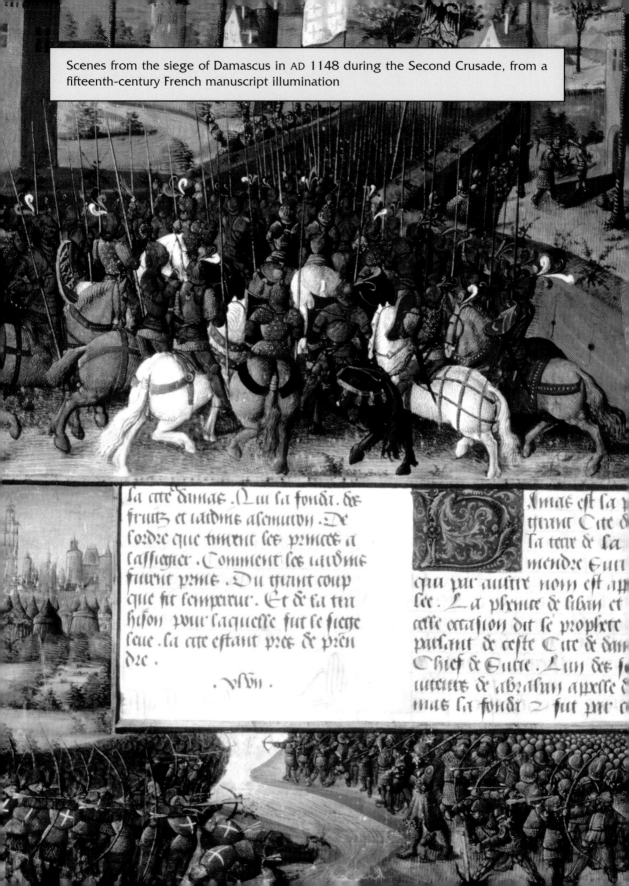

Scenes from the siege of Damascus in AD 1148 during the Second Crusade, from a fifteenth-century French manuscript illumination

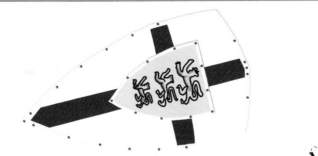

The First Crusades

The land of Palestine came under the rule of the Muslims in the seventh century, when the Arab followers of Muhammad swept northward from Mecca, conquering the eastern Mediterranean countries. Although the Muslims occupied Jerusalem, they still allowed Christian pilgrims to enter the country and visit the holy places linked with Jesus.

Unfortunately, this tolerance came to a dramatic end in the eleventh century when a much fiercer Muslim ruler, Malik Shah, leader of the Seljuk Turks, defeated the Christian Byzantine army at the Battle of Manzikert in AD 1071 and swiftly moved southward to occupy Syria and the whole of Palestine. Byzantium, also known as Constantinople, and nowadays called Istanbul, had been the richest and most powerful city in the East for many centuries. The Byzantine Empire had always seemed invincible, so the destruction of its army at Manzikert came as a crushing blow. Shortly afterward, when the Seljuks occupied Jerusalem and slaughtered the Christians, the shock waves were felt throughout Europe.

In desperation, the Byzantine emperor begged the pope, Urban II, to muster an army from the Christian countries in Europe to prevent the Turks from making any further advances and especially to rescue Jerusalem from its fierce Muslim occupants. Pope Urban II took on the challenge. He was a brilliant orator, and in 1095 at Clermont in France, he made an impassioned speech urging Christians to unite in a holy war against the Turks. He described the atrocities that were taking place and proclaimed that "a race alien to God has invaded the land of those Christians, has reduced the people with sword and flame, and has carried off some as captives to its own lands."

"Christ himself will be your leader!" the pope continued. "Wear his cross as your badge! If you are killed, all your sins will be pardoned!" It was an inspiring speech, and everyone present gave a great shout of "God wills it!" News of this great enterprise spread like wildfire throughout Europe, and as a result the First Crusade was planned, with knights and princes from different countries taking part.

The word "crusade" derives from the Latin *crux*, meaning "cross," and those taking part were encouraged to sew cross-shaped pieces of cloth onto their tunics.

But even before the knights could get themselves assembled, a strange-looking monk called Peter the Hermit roused tens of thousands of ordinary people—men, women, and children—to join him in setting off for Constantinople on the way to Jerusalem. Peter was a fascinating person—ugly, indescribably dirty, barefoot, riding a donkey, and wearing a filthy monk's habit and a hermit's cloak. The rabble who followed him regarded him as almost divine and even grabbed hairs from

A crusader and a Moor in combat, from a twelfth-century Italian mosaic. The Moors were Muslims from North Africa who invaded Spain in the eighth century and retained control of parts of Spain as late as the fifteenth century.

the tail of his donkey as sacred relics. This "People's Crusade," as it came to be called, struggled across Europe and actually reached Constantinople, but Peter and his followers were a disorganized mob without any military expertise or weapons, and they were completely wiped out, massacred by the Turks near Nicaea almost a year after setting out.

The Capture of Jerusalem

In 1096, following soon after Peter the Hermit's ill-fated adventure, many princes and knights and their armies from various parts of Europe equipped themselves with horses, armor, and weapons and traveled by different routes to Constantinople. From there the combined forces planned to move south through Turkish-held Anatolia and then down the coast of the Holy Land to Jerusalem itself.

From France came three brothers: Godfrey of Bouillon; Eustace, count of Boulogne; and Baldwin of Boulogne. From Normandy came Robert, the eldest son of William the Conqueror, and his cousin, another Robert, count of Flanders. Raymond IV, count of Toulouse, brought the largest army. He had already lost an eye fighting the Moors in Spain. Then there was Bohemond, prince of Taranto in southern Italy, and Henry, count of Vermandois, who only just managed to get to Constantinople after having been shipwrecked on the way and losing most of his followers. The bishop of Le Puy, who was the official representative of the pope, was the designated religious leader of the combined Christian armies.

Antioch, the third largest city in the old Roman Empire, was the gateway to the Holy Land, so the crusaders had to capture this city before they could go farther south to Jerusalem. After a siege of nearly nine months and with help from spies within the walls, a scaling party managed to climb up the walls and seize the town. The governor's head was presented to Bohemond as a trophy of war.

Meanwhile, Baldwin of Boulogne succeeded in capturing the strategically important city of Edessa. He married a local princess and became its ruler. The surrounding territory became the first crusader settlement, known as the County of Edessa.

Quarrels quickly broke out among the crusaders who had taken Antioch, as they argued about what to do next. Bohemond was determined to hold on to his position as ruler of Antioch, so he remained behind while the others pressed on to Jerusalem. In this way Antioch now became the second crusader settlement, to be known as the Principality of Antioch.

It was left to the one-eyed Raymond of Toulouse to lead the armies on to Marra, the next city south on the way to Jerusalem. Having won a victory there, he led his men barefoot as a pilgrim for the last three hundred miles to the Holy City. The siege of Jerusalem lasted just five weeks, and ingenious new siege engines and trebuchet catapults were used in the last assault. There was appalling bloodshed as the crusaders finally slaughtered their way into the city. Synagogues were burned with people imprisoned inside. Treasure was looted. The massacre of the Jewish and Muslim inhabitants was so terrible that the bishop of Pisa wrote back to the pope saying, "If you desire to know what was done with the enemy . . . our men rode in the blood of Saracens up to the knees of their horses."

Thus, in July 1099, the first crusaders celebrated a bloody victory and set up the new Kingdom of Jerusalem, with Godfrey of Bouillon as its first ruler.

The Rise of Saladin

At first sight, the capture of Jerusalem by the crusaders in 1099 may seem to have brought the holy war to a successful

PORTRAIT OF SALADIN (?)

FATIMID SCHOOL

About A.D. 1180

A portrait of Salah-ed-Din Yusuf, better known as Saladin, who became caliph of Egypt in 1169 and by 1174 had united all the Muslims of Egypt and Syria under his rule

conclusion. However, the Crusades were to last for another two centuries. Owing to the determination of the leaders of the First Crusade to keep the territory they had conquered for themselves, four separate crusader states had come into being at the beginning of the twelfth century.

In the north was the landlocked County of Edessa. Farther south was the Principality of Antioch, which had good access to the Mediterranean. Still farther south was the smaller state called the County of Tripoli, also on the coast. And finally came the largest and most important state, the Kingdom of Jerusalem, which possessed many coastal ports, with the Muslim caliphate of Egypt on its southern borders. Together, these new states came to be known as Outremer, which is French for "overseas." However, the four states of Outremer were never properly united, and there was constant friction between them and struggles to gain power whenever one of their rulers died or was killed. As time went on, more recruits from Europe were needed to maintain the necessary defenses in each of these separate states.

In essence, these Outremer states comprised a long coastal strip of Christian territory surrounded by Muslims on three sides. The Christian rulers were vastly outnumbered, and of course there were countless battles and skirmishes. At last, in 1144, disaster struck, and Edessa was recaptured by Muslim Turks led by a powerful leader named Zengi.

Clearly a new call to arms was needed. Although Louis VII of France and Conrad III of Germany joined forces to mount the Second Crusade, this was a complete disaster for the Christians. The crusader armies were completely routed by Zengi's son, Nur-ed-Din. For the next forty years, Outremer became weaker, while the Muslims, united by their new champion, Nur-ed-Din, became stronger and stronger.

Then, in 1174, Outremer was to face an even more powerful opponent, Salah-ed-Din Yusuf, better known to future historians as Saladin. Son of one of Nur-ed-Din's generals, Saladin had become the ruler of Egypt in 1169. He quickly gained more and more influence and power until finally in 1174, on the death of Nur-ed-Din, he proclaimed himself Nur-ed-Din's successor, thus bringing Syria and Egypt under one ruler.

If only the rulers of the Outremer states had swiftly united at this time, they might have defeated Saladin, but the moment

Saladin's army, from a fourteenth-century French illuminated manuscript. The Muslim warriors are depicted with turbans and beards.

was lost. The various crusader leaders were constantly arguing with each other. At last, when Guy of Lusignan became king of Jerusalem in 1186, he became so alarmed at the growing threat posed by Saladin to the crusader kingdoms that he decided to assemble the Christian knights together and challenge Saladin once and for all in battle

The Loss of Jerusalem

In June 1187, Saladin invaded Galilee and besieged the city of Tiberias (nowadays called Teverya). It was an open challenge to the Christian forces, especially as the wife of Count Raymond of Tripoli was trapped inside.

The Christian leaders argued whether to attack immediately or to conserve their strength and wait at Acre for Saladin's next move. The more cautious leaders believed that Saladin's troops would exhaust themselves if they were forced to do all the marching and attacking, especially in the extreme heat of the Palestine summer. However, the Christians, led by Guy of Lusignan, made the foolish decision to march their comparatively small army toward Saladin. It was a major error in judgment.

The Christians set off from Acre before dawn and suffered desperate thirst as they marched all day in the scorching desert. By late afternoon, they reached a hill with twin peaks known as the Horns of Hattin. King Guy decided to camp there for the night. Some of his followers begged him to press on to the lake of Galilee, just five miles away, but he stubbornly refused to listen.

The following morning, the Christian army found itself completely surrounded by Saladin's army. Worse still, blinding smoke was blowing into their eyes as the Muslims had lit bonfires around them. Disoriented, surprised, desperate with thirst, and completely outnumbered, the result was inevitable. In the ensuing daylong battle, the Christian army was completely annihilated, and King Guy was taken prisoner.

It is impossible to exaggerate the importance of the Battle of Hattin. After this victory, Saladin was able to take town after town throughout Outremer until, in October 1187, after a short siege, he led his army into Jerusalem itself. Unlike the

Saladin's army attacks and captures Jerusalem in AD 1187, from an early-fifteenth-century French manuscript. Here the Saracens are depicted in the same way as western European knights.

slaughter and bloodshed that had accompanied the fall of Jerusalem to the crusaders in 1099—eighty-eight years earlier—Saladin gave orders that this time there should be no massacre or looting. Christians would not be molested but were allowed to ransom themselves for a fairly small sum. Saladin was a fierce and powerful commander in battle but generous in victory. The poor were allowed their freedom for nothing.

By the end of 1187 then, the crusader kingdom of Jerusalem had virtually ceased to exist. The Christians still

The Horns of Hattin, a series of hills south of the city of Acre, where Saladin's forces surrounded and destroyed a crusader army in AD 1187, enabling the Muslims to recapture Jerusalem in the same year

managed to hold on in just three towns—Tyre, Antioch, and Tripoli. And they still held five castles, including the mighty Krak des Chevaliers. However, these were only toeholds.

Naturally enough, the entire Christian world was horrified to hear of the fall of Jerusalem. The pope himself, Urban III, already a sick man, died of shock. Inevitably, there would have to be yet another Crusade. In November 1187, a month after Saladin's great victory, the first European prince to "take the cross" was Richard of England. Richard was not yet king,

The ruins of the Krak des Chevaliers crusader castle in Syria, one of the few strongholds the Christians were able to hold on to after the fall of Jerusalem to Saladin in AD 1187

but when he came to the throne shortly afterward, such was his resolve that in December 1189, just three months after his coronation, he left England to make his way to the Holy Land.

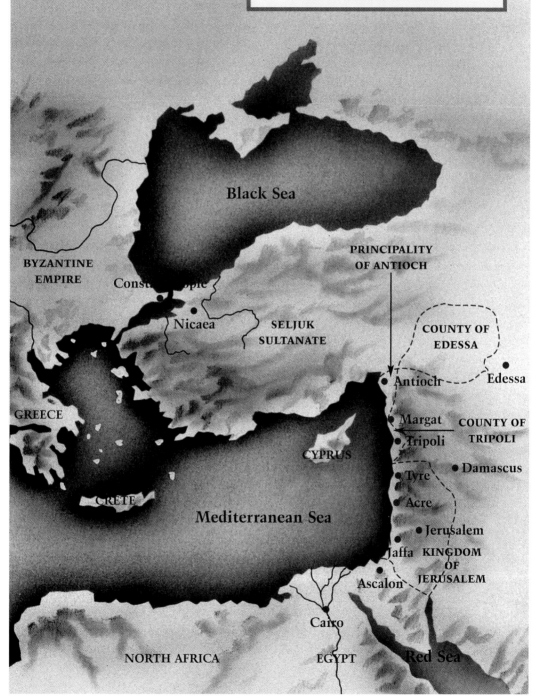

ASIA MINOR AND THE
MIDDLE EAST AT THE TIME
OF THE CRUSADES

Black Sea

BYZANTINE
EMPIRE

Constantinople

Nicaea

SELJUK
SULTANATE

PRINCIPALITY
OF ANTIOCH

COUNTY OF
EDESSA

Antioch

Edessa

GREECE

Margat

COUNTY OF
TRIPOLI

Tripoli

CYPRUS

Damascus

Tyre

CRETE

Acre

Mediterranean Sea

Jerusalem

Jaffa

KINGDOM
OF
JERUSALEM

Ascalon

Cairo

NORTH AFRICA

EGYPT

Red Sea

Frederick I, known as Barbarossa ("Redbeard"), king of Germany and Holy Roman emperor, dressed as a crusader. He was one of the three kings who led the Third Crusade.

A New Crusade

Twice before, a pope had called the leaders of Europe to mount a Crusade. This time, in 1187, it was Pope Gregory VIII who made the usual promise that all those who "took the cross" would be assured of a place in Heaven, and that all their sins would be forgiven. Taking the cross meant that a prince or knight would solemnly be given a piece of cloth in the shape of a cross to be sewn on to his surcoat, the tunic he wore over his armor. Further benefits given to crusaders included postponement of the repayment of any debts they owed until they returned. The church also promised to protect their property while they were away. However, it was the spirit of adventure and the chance to travel and fight in a holy war that spurred most of the young knights. Life was often boring at home, and stories of the rich lifestyle to be found in the Eastern countries were spreading in the West.

Three kings decided to take their armies to confront Saladin: Richard I, the newly crowned king of England, aged thirty-two; King Philip Augustus of France, aged twenty-four; and the great German emperor, Frederick

Barbarossa, known as Redbeard, aged nearly seventy, who had already been on the throne for more than thirty years. It was Frederick Barbarossa who set off first. He had a tremendous reputation for bravery and military skill. He had assembled the largest army ever to leave Europe, consisting of about twenty thousand knights, probably even more infantrymen, and at least six thousand camp followers. These figures may be exaggerated, but it is clear that a huge army left Regensburg, Germany, in May 1189.

Frederick marched through Hungary toward Constantinople, where the Byzantine emperor panicked, thinking that the German army was about to attack his city, and refused to let them enter. In turn, Frederick believed that the Byzantines were his enemies, and he sent for reinforcements. After defeating the Byzantine army, it was nearly winter, so Frederick decided to wait at Adrianople before continuing south. Then, the following spring, marching through Anatolia, he was confronted by Seljuk Turks and fought another victorious battle at Iconium.

All now seemed well for his Crusade as he moved toward Tarsus. The journey had been difficult, but at last he was nearing the northernmost territory of Outremer and was within reach of Antioch, one of the cities still held by Christians. Then tragedy struck. In June 1190, as he was crossing a river, Frederick Barbarossa slipped from his saddle and drowned. The Germans had lost their leader, and they were completely demoralized. They carried Redbeard's corpse, preserved in vinegar, back to Antioch. Many soldiers returned to Germany, and just a pitiful few struggled on to Acre to join Guy of Lusignan there. Obviously

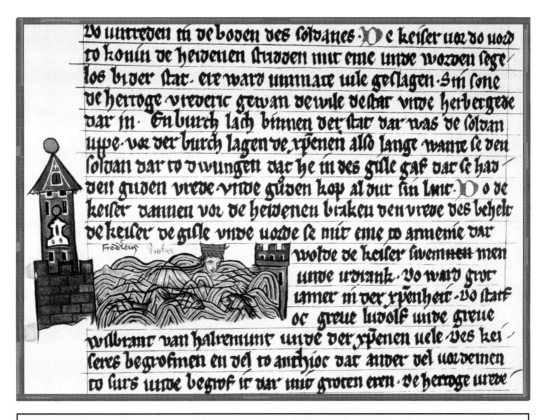

The death of Frederick I, from a thirteenth-century German manuscript. In June 1190 he drowned while trying to cross a river in Turkey. His army became demoralized and eventually broke up.

the Third Crusade was going to have to wait for the arrival of Richard I and Philip Augustus.

Richard and Philip Augustus

In July 1190, just one month after the death of Frederick Barbarossa, the two other European kings, Richard of England and Philip Augustus of France, set off from Vezelay in France, taking different routes to Messina in Sicily, from where they planned to sail to the Holy Land.

The coronation of King Richard I of England, from a fifteenth-century French manuscript

Richard the Lionheart and the Third Crusade

At this time Richard and Philip were great friends. Both of them were young and unmarried, and they had already been allies in waging war against Richard's father, Henry II. Their temperaments were different, however. Philip, blind in one eye, had no real love of fighting, being quieter and more of a diplomat than Richard. Richard, by everyone's accounts, was a man of superb physique, tall, incredibly handsome, strong, and talented in the arts of poetry and music as well as in the skills of battle. He had unbounded energy and a ferocious and violent temper. Normally he was generous and courteous, but his moods were unpredictable and he could be callous and cruel. Above all, he was a natural leader, and he adored the excitement of war. He had acquired his nickname, Coeur de Lion, or "Lionheart," because of his bravery in combat.

However, there were tensions between the two kings, because Richard had inherited a larger part of France than Philip himself possessed. They had agreed to go on a crusade together partly because they did not trust each other not to invade each other's kingdoms if one of them were to go alone. On the surface, however, they were allies. Richard was even engaged to Philip's sister, Alice. Richard's sister Joanna had been the wife of King William of Sicily, who had just died. Arriving in Sicily, Richard was furious to discover that his sister Joanna was being ill-treated by Tancred, the new ruler of the island. In his rage, Richard seized the city of Messina, releasing it only on payment of a large sum of gold. Meanwhile, his mother, Eleanor of Aquitaine, arrived on the island bringing Princess Berengaria of Navarre with her. She was Eleanor's choice of an alternative bride for Richard!

From her grave site in France, the stone effigy of Eleanor of Aquitaine, wife of Henry II and mother of Richard I

Faced with all this, it was only natural that King Philip would be thoroughly irritated. He had no part in the row with Tancred, and now his own sister, Alice, was being rejected as Richard's future wife. Philip felt snubbed and humiliated, and the friendship between the kings was almost at the breaking point.

In March 1191, Philip set sail for Acre, and Richard's fleet followed soon after, with Berengaria and Joanna sailing together in a separate ship. This ship was blown off course near Cyprus and had to shelter in Limassol Bay. The unsympathetic

An illustration from a fifteenth-century French manuscript depicts *(above)* the French crusaders of King Philip Augustus boarding ships for Acre and *(below)* Richard's English fleet attacking a Saracen warship.

ruler of Cyprus not only refused them permission to land but also denied them water and food supplies. Naturally, when Richard heard of this, he flew into one of his notorious rages, conquered the whole island, imprisoned its ruler, and installed a couple of Englishmen as governors. He married Berengaria in Limassol and pressed on to join Philip in Palestine, arriving at Acre on July 8, 1191. At last the Third Crusade was about to begin.

The Siege of Acre

When Richard arrived off the coast of Palestine, he found that the Muslim city of Acre was already being besieged by the combined forces of the Christians, led by King Guy of

Jerusalem. Saladin, it will be remembered, had captured Guy after the Battle of Hattin and could easily have put him to death there and then. However, Saladin was a man of honor who always treated his enemies with courtesy and had never been known to break his word.

After being so soundly defeated in battle, Guy had been set free by Saladin on the condition that he leave the country. Guy had given his solemn promise to Saladin that he would return to France, but on gaining his freedom he immediately asked the church to release him from his promise, arguing that it had only been made to a Muslim! As soon as he was free, Guy gathered up what remained of his army and tried at first to enter Tyre. Its ruler, Conrad of Montferrat, not only refused him entry but also refused to recognize him as king. Guy therefore decided to march farther south and attack Acre. Later, this bitter rivalry between Conrad and Guy was to have far-reaching consequences.

Now, camped outside the walls of Acre, Guy had been somewhat ineffectually besieging the city for almost two years. He commanded a small but growing army composed of the remnants of the troops who had fought at Hattin, the remnants of Frederick Barbarossa's German army, and rein-forcements recently arrived in Outremer, including Leopold V, duke of Austria, with his own separate army. Even Conrad of Montferrat had come to help, as, of course, did Philip Augustus of France, who had recently arrived from Sicily with his army. Together, Guy and Philip had begun making siege engines to mount a final attack.

Watching the siege and, in fact, besieging the besiegers, Saladin and his army had camped nearby, but

A crusader army arrives in the Holy Land and occupies a Muslim city, from a fifteenth-century French illustration.

Guy's position was so well chosen that Saladin could do little to impede the constant bombardments of the city. Meanwhile, the Muslims within the city used carrier pigeons to communicate with Saladin.

The arrival of Richard with twenty-five ships filled with troops, supplies, and weapons gave a huge boost to the besiegers' morale, and it brought despair to the six thousand Muslims trapped inside the walls of Acre. Quite apart from facing the additional forces now arrayed against them, the Muslims were completely blockaded from the sea, and they were desperate for food. Such was the power of Richard's personality that it was automatically assumed that he was now in charge of military operations. Although for a while he was ill, he quickly took charge of directing the bombardments and erected his huge portable wooden castle, named Mategriffon, right in front of the city gate.

Within a few weeks of Richard's arrival in the Holy Land, after suffering an intense bombardment by stones from the crusaders' catapults, the besieged Muslims in Acre surrendered. The terms of surrender called for those within the city to be spared for a ransom of 200,000 gold pieces. Fifteen hundred Christian prisoners held by Saladin were to be released. A piece of the Holy Cross, captured by Saladin at the Battle of Hattin, was to be returned. With wild delight the victorious contingents of the crusader armies swarmed into Acre.

An incident now occurred that was to have enormous consequences. Exulting in their triumph, the English and French troops ran up their banners over the city as a sign of victory. Not to be outdone, Duke Leopold of Austria planted his own banner side by side with those of England and France. Leopold's army, of course, was much smaller than those of Philip or Richard, and it had played a relatively insignificant part in capturing the city. Therefore, when

A squire is knighted by the King, from a fourteenth century manuscript illumination.

English soldiers saw Leopold's banners flying alongside their own, they took matters into their own hands and tore them down, throwing them into a ditch. Naturally, Leopold was deeply offended, even more so when he complained to Richard and nothing was done about it. It was an unendurable insult, so he left Acre immediately and returned to Austria, seething with anger.

Richard hardly concerned himself over Leopold's departure, for there were other troubles on his mind. No sooner had the combined armies gained their victory than a serious argument broke out over who would be king of Jerusalem when the city was taken. King Guy considered himself still to be king, and he was supported by Richard. However, Conrad of Montferrat was also claiming to be king, and he was supported by King Philip of France, who felt that Guy had forfeited his right to be king after his disastrous defeat at Hattin. Conrad was the lord of Tyre who had refused to acknowledge Guy when he had come to him after being released from captivity by Saladin.

It was a tricky political problem and various groups took different sides. A compromise was reached whereby Guy would remain king, but on his death the throne would pass to Conrad or any son of his. Reluctantly, Philip put up with this compromise, but he was getting tired of the whole enterprise and decided it was time to go home. He sailed out of Acre on July 31, 1191, thus leaving Richard in sole command.

By now Richard was getting impatient, feeling that Saladin was taking too long in releasing prisoners and paying the ransom money. He set Saladin a time limit, and when this wasn't met, he committed the most barbaric act of his life. He ordered almost one thousand citizens of Acre—men, women, and children—to be led out of the city, where he had them all publicly slaughtered in full view of the encamped Muslim army. It was an appalling scene of butchery that his opponents would never forget.

Archers attack a Muslim fortress, all drawn within this initial letter from a fourteenth-century French manuscript.

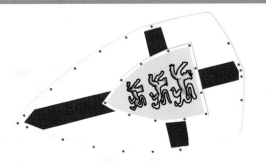

The Armies Arrive at Jerusalem

our days after the terrible massacre of Muslim prisoners outside the walls of Acre, Richard gathered his armies together and marched south. He was determined to free Jerusalem from Saladin's control, and now that he was in full and undisputed command of the Christian forces, he was keen to act quickly. It can be seen from a map what he now had to do. Clearly, his main target was Jerusalem itself. But Jerusalem lay inland, and strung out along the coast were a number of important towns—all fortified— that would first have to be overcome or bypassed. Richard's plan was to reach Jaffa and then move inland to the Holy City. Marching south, Richard had the sea on his right, and the Muslim forces did what they could to harass and delay him on his left.

The route was dusty. The heat of the sun was ferocious. Despite their weariness and thirst, the crusaders had to keep up with their leaders or else be killed by the watchful enemy. Everywhere they found that Saladin's forces had been there before them and had destroyed crops and razed buildings and fortresses.

This sixth-century mosaic image of the city of Jerusalem was made sometime after the collapse of the Roman Empire. The city's fortified wall can be seen.

After about two weeks, on September 7, 1191, the crusaders were approaching the coastal city of Arsuf, about sixty miles from Acre, when they suddenly found Saladin's men drawn up in battle lines, blocking the way ahead. It has been calculated that the Muslim army consisted of about eighty thousand soldiers, whereas Richard's combined armies were only a third as large. Nevertheless, Richard's superb military skill was to win the day.

Richard arranged his army in tight formation, with his knights on their heavy horses in the middle and the bowmen in front of them. Wave after wave of Muslim warriors, mounted on light, swift horses, charged at the crusader army but failed to penetrate its ranks. They were repulsed by showers of arrows that could easily pierce their thin armor. Richard waited and took his time judging the appropriate moment to charge. His commanders begged him to give the order, but Richard would not be rushed.

Two of Richard's knights could wait no longer and began to charge. Instantly Richard took the lead, having no alternative, and luckily for him the power and force of the huge French and English horses and the ferocity of the knights with their immensely long lances combined to scatter the Muslim armies in terror. A contemporary account describes Richard's own part in the battle. "There the King, the fierce, the extraordinary King, cut down the Turks in every direction, and none could escape the force of his arm, for wherever he turned, brandishing his sword, he carved a wide path for himself, cutting them down like a reaper with his sickle."

At the end of the day Richard had won an impressive victory, suffering few losses and gaining a formidable reputation for invincibility. Three days later, he reached Jaffa.

Truce Talks

Saladin had now suffered two defeats—at Acre and at Arsuf—and his troops were demoralized. However, his losses at Arsuf were fewer than he had feared, so the actual balance of power between the two opposing armies had not greatly changed. Saladin settled his troops in Jerusalem, expecting Richard to march to the Holy City as soon as he was ready.

Richard arrived at Jaffa only to find that it was in ruins. He had to camp in an olive grove outside the city, while his men repaired the fortifications and made it a safe haven for his supply ships. This would take some time, but Richard was glad to be able to give his troops a rest from fighting. Jaffa was valuable, but more important strategically was the great harbor-fortress of Ascalon, which lay on the road between Egypt and Syria about sixty miles farther south along the coast. Richard realized the importance of Ascalon, but for the moment he did not feel able to stir his men for further action.

Saladin also realized the importance of Ascalon, and his next move was quite extraordinary. He took a contingent of his army to Ascalon and ordered this prosperous town to be totally demolished, stone by stone. Desperately the inhabitants pleaded with him not to destroy their city, but Saladin was adamant that it should not fall into the hands of the Christians. "I would rather lose all my children," he declared, "than cast a stone from its walls, but it is necessary."

The situation between the two opposing forces was now something of a stalemate. Richard's army was enjoying a relatively easy life in Jaffa, and Richard himself had even brought his newly wedded wife, Berengaria, and his sister, Joanna, to share his luxuries. It was now that Richard began to think it was time for negotiations. He sent envoys to Saladin, who agreed, and soon a lengthy period of truce

A depiction of Richard and Saladin in individual combat, from a fourteenth-century English prayer book. Saladin admired Richard, regarding him as extremely brave, but he also thought him reckless and capable of great cruelty.

talks began between Richard and Adil Saif-ed-Din (Safadin), Saladin's brother.

Surprisingly, these talks were held in a cordial and friendly atmosphere. One proposal that Richard made was that Safadin himself should marry Richard's sister Joanna, and the pair of them would live in Jerusalem, giving free access to Christians! He even went on to suggest that Safadin himself should become a Christian. But the truce talks were not successful. So in November, Richard started to march toward Jerusalem. The weather was so bad that when he was only twelve miles from the city he decided to pull back. He decided instead to spend the winter rebuilding Ascalon, the city that had just been demolished by Saladin. It would give him a solid base from which to prevent any Muslim rein-forcements reaching Saladin from Egypt.

Then, at last, in June 1192, Richard set off from Ascalon on what everyone hoped would be the final attack on Jerusalem.

Jerusalem the Unattainable

Richard's men must have rejoiced when they began to feel that their great enterprise of rescuing Jerusalem was now coming to a climax. In the middle of June 1192, they reached the town of Beit Nuba, only twelve miles from Jerusalem. This was the place they had reached the previous winter, and here, once again, Richard set up camp and halted.

For three weeks Richard waited and pondered his next move. Unlike his troops, he was in a somber mood, for the more he thought about his position the more he realized that he was in a no-win situation. He was a great military tactician, and he knew that he would never succeed. For one thing, Jerusalem was extremely well fortified and strongly garrisoned, with Saladin himself in command. The route from Beit Nuba would be difficult, and there would be very little food or water for his troops even if he began to besiege Jerusalem. Richard knew, too, that he simply did not have the required number of men, and in any case a siege would probably last months, by which time he would almost certainly be cut off from the sea by another Muslim army.

As he thought about the future, even more problems presented themselves in his mind. Suppose that he did take Jerusalem? What then? He certainly didn't have enough men to hold the city indefinitely without constant reinforcements of soldiers and equipment. He could not rely on the other leaders of the Outremer states, who were

The Judean Hills, looking west toward Jerusalem. This is the kind of terrain the crusaders marched through in full armor.

too busy squabbling among themselves and struggling to maintain their own little kingdoms.

Richard also knew that once his men had captured Jerusalem most of them would want to go home and he wouldn't be able to stop them. After all, they had served him well and had undergone immense hardships. They didn't want to settle there for the rest of their lives. Richard himself did not want to stay away from England any longer, for he had heard news that his brother John was seizing too much power in his absence. And then there was Philip Augustus of France, who had already returned home. Who could know what trouble he would be stirring up in Richard's possessions in Normandy and Aquitaine?

It is said that during this period of anguished thinking, Richard rode out one day to a hilltop near Emmaus, where Jerusalem was visible in the distance, with its towers and

An aerial view of what remains today of the central citadel of the city of Jerusalem. It was captured by the first crusaders in AD 1099 and recaptured by the Saracens under Saladin in AD 1187.

domes glinting in the sun. Richard knew it was there and covered his face so that he could not see it. It was so near, so precious, so desirable, and yet so unattainable. It is to Richard's credit that, despite his eagerness for conquest, he recognized that a deadlock had arisen. Although it would be difficult and humiliating to order his men away from

Jerusalem for the second time, he made up his mind to retreat. However, an unexpected diversion was about to occur.

The Battle of Jaffa

As Richard was preparing to announce his decision to retreat, some exciting news arrived. A lengthy caravan of oxcarts and camels was reported to be moving toward them, bringing supplies to Saladin from Egypt. Richard couldn't believe his good fortune, and legend has it that at night he dressed himself as an Arab and secretly rode out to inspect it for himself, almost falling into Muslim hands when challenged by sentries, or guards. The next day, Richard's army fell on the defenseless caravan, capturing everyone and everything—food, wine, weapons of war, more than a thousand horses, and almost as many camels. The crusaders were overjoyed as they divided the booty.

Again Richard asked Saladin for peace negotiations, and agreement was almost in sight, except that the future of Ascalon was proving to be a stumbling block. Richard was so sure of reaching a settlement, however, that he left Jaffa and traveled north to Acre, ready to depart by ship for England. With Richard's departure, the opportunity to seize Jaffa was too great a temptation for Saladin, and he swooped on the city, taking it by surprise.

Hearing this, Richard immediately sailed from Acre back to Jaffa, leaving his army to catch up with him after marching south by land. As soon as Richard's fleet arrived off the coast of Jaffa, a priest jumped from the city wall, ran to the beach, and swam out to Richard's galley to tell him the latest news. Richard reacted with boldness and speed, ordering his sailors

A battle between crusaders and Muslims, from a fourteenth-century French manuscript

to row their ships to the beach and ground them. He leapt onto the beach and led his men with such ferocity that the Muslim forces fled frantically into the desert. Thus Jaffa was recaptured.

Saladin was angry to learn that his troops had been defeated by such a small force, and he was determined to retake Jaffa at the earliest opportunity. Within a few days, he silently approached the city at night, ready to attack the next morning.

Unfortunately for Saladin, his army was spotted, so that at daybreak Richard's tiny army was ready for him. The battle that followed was quite astonishing. Richard had only fifty-four knights and fifteen horses. He also had about two thousand infantrymen and a contingent of skilled English archers. He grouped his forces in tight formation and allowed wave after wave of Muslim horsemen to attack. At last he unleashed a great volley of arrows, and then, mounted on one of the horses, he personally led a charge against the enemy, just as they were reeling from the volley of arrows. It was a spectacular display of daring, and Richard's horse was killed under him. In a memorable gesture of admiration, Saladin himself ordered fresh horses to be led, under a flag of truce, and presented to Richard, with his compliments.

Thus, against all odds, the battle of Jaffa was won, and Saladin withdrew his forces to the safety of Jerusalem.

Four English kings, from a thirteenth-century English manuscript. Top left is Henry II, Richard's father. Top right, with the sword, is Richard I. Bottom left is John I, Richard's brother, who succeeded him. Bottom right is Henry III, John's son.

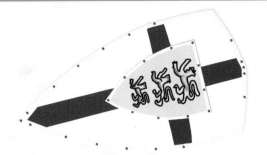

Richard Leaves the Holy Land

The Battle of Jaffa proved to be Richard's last military exploit in the Holy Land. It had been a dazzling display of determination, skill, and courage, outstanding even in a lifetime of incessant warfare. However, after the Battle of Jaffa, Richard was anxious to return to England, especially when he learned that his brother John was plotting against him with the help of the French. For Richard, it was now necessary to sign a peace treaty with Saladin, and Saladin himself was keen to be rid of this extraordinary golden-haired opponent. He did not want to be constantly at war. In any case, at this time both he and Richard fell ill.

The two leaders exchanged gifts of fruit and medicine. Then, on September 2, 1192, an agreement was signed that was to last for three years. Jerusalem was to remain in Muslim hands, but Christian pilgrims were to be allowed free access to the holy places there, as well as to Bethlehem and Nazareth. All the lands of Outremer were still to be held by the Christian settlers, including the important coastal cities from Tyre to Jaffa. Also, the Principality of Antioch and the County of Tripoli were to remain in

Christian hands. However, as for Ascalon, this city was to be demolished again, for Saladin was utterly determined not to let this strategically important fortress fall into Christian hands again. Richard could not budge him on this.

The fighting was over, and Richard was free to visit Jerusalem, but he had no heart to enter the city except as a conqueror. Instead, he rested a while at Acre, recovering his health, and then, at last, on October 9, 1192, he set sail for home. The Muslim people must have breathed a great sigh of relief, for he had gained a formidable reputation for ruthlessness and near invincibility. For centuries afterward, Muslim mothers would quiet their naughty children by warning them that the great Malik Ric would come and get them!

As for Saladin, he must have realized that the continued existence of crusader cities and castles along the coast would pose a future threat if Richard or other militant crusaders were ever to return. However, he was a man of his word, and Christians were grateful to be allowed to make their pilgrimages in guaranteed safety. Richard was destined never to go back to the Holy Land again, although he frequently expressed his intention of doing so. His great opponent Saladin was to survive only a few months after Richard's departure. Saladin died in Damascus on March 3, 1193, aged fifty-four.

In such a manner, the Third Crusade came to an end. In some respects it may appear to have been a failure, but Richard had paved the way for a short period of relative peace, as he turned his attention to his problems in England. He had been away from his kingdom for almost three years, and it was now time to return home.

Richard in Prison

Richard set sail from Acre on October 9, 1192, having already sent his wife, Berengaria, ahead of him. Little did he know of the difficulties now awaiting him. A heavy gale blew up shortly after his fleet had left port, and Richard's galley became separated from the other ships. From then on, for months, no one knew where he was. It seemed probable that he had drowned.

In fact, what happened was that as he neared the south coast of France he learned that he would be in danger of capture, and he certainly didn't want to fall into the hands of his rival, Philip Augustus. He decided to turn back, sail up the Adriatic, and find an overland route through Germany. All went well until he reached Corfu, where he was attacked by pirates. At first he fought them off, but as his boat was damaged he came to terms with them, offering them good payment if they would take him farther. Then the pirate boat itself was shipwrecked on the coast between Venice and Aquileia. Richard now found himself in territory controlled by one of his political enemies, the German emperor, Henry VI. The situation called for caution.

History mingles with legend at this point, with Richard taking up various disguises and narrowly avoiding capture by pretending to be either a pilgrim, a merchant, or even a kitchen servant. One story tells how he was roasting meat on a spit when his real identity was given away because he was wearing a suspiciously valuable ring. Whatever the truth may be, he managed to get as far as Vienna, hoping to reach friends in Moravia. But then, just before Christmas 1192, he

pres henry le secund regna Richard sun fiz. r. aunze
denip fi entre papiza and de la terre seynt fuist puf del duly
te oftere par eyde del roy phylipe de fraunce e fuist teynt hors
de pafon pur cent mil lyucres de argent e pur cel raumeum fu
tent les chalis de Englectere pris. des Egyptes e vendus. puis
fust tret de vn quarel de Alblast al chastel de Chalezun. dite
cete vers fu fer: Xpe tui calicis: predo fit preda calicis.

This illustration from a thirteenth-century English manuscript shows the arrest and confinement of Richard I. The duke of Austria arrested him in Vienna in December 1192.

fell into the hands of Leopold of Austria.

This was the same Leopold who had left the Crusade in a fury after his banners had been torn down at Acre by English soldiers. Now, his revenge would be sweet! Richard was imprisoned in Dürnstein Castle on the banks of the Danube. The castle ruins can still be seen by tourists who travel by boat to Vienna. The most famous legend of all tells how Richard's minstrel, the faithful Blondel, having searched the length and breadth of Austria, came to sing Richard's own compositions under these walls and was rewarded by hearing Richard's own voice joining in.

Eager to make money, Leopold sold Richard for 75,000 marks to Henry VI, emperor of Germany, who took his new captive to Speyer to haggle over Richard's future. Eventually Henry demanded the enormous sum of 100,000 marks (about thirty-four tons of silver) from England as ransom, plus the loan of fifty galleys and one hundred knights for a year. Back in England it took a quarter of every man's income for a whole year to raise the necessary ransom money. Pigs were killed, sheep shorn, church valuables sold. It was an expensive business rescuing Richard, but eventually he arrived back in England on March 14, 1194, to a tumultuous welcome.

Richard's Life After the Crusade

Richard's formidable old mother, Eleanor of Aquitaine, helped to raise the necessary ransom. She had been on the Second Crusade herself with her first husband, King Louis of France. She was now anxious that her son Richard should be restored to kingly dignity in England, for it was considered something of a dishonor to have suffered imprisonment. Richard was therefore given a second coronation in Winchester Cathedral.

Richard's first act was to confront his younger brother, John, who had acted treasonably during his absence. He could have punished John severely, but he acted with generosity and made light of John's disloyalty, treating him with playful contempt. Meanwhile, he appointed a trusted adviser, Hubert Walter, archbishop of Canterbury, to act as his deputy, especially whenever he was out of the country.

Next, Richard now had to defend his possessions in France, for Philip Augustus had been invading and occupying English-held lands in France. It was the perfect excuse to leave England once again and embark on what would be another never-ending succession of sieges, skirmishes,

The stone effigy of King Richard I from his grave site in France

and battles. Richard's struggle against the French armies of Philip Augustus was to last for another six years. There were many triumphs. Typically, in one of his letters back to Hubert Walter, he mentioned that he had just seized the town of Angoulême "in a single evening" and "captured full 300 knights and 40,000 men-at-arms."

One day, as he was besieging another French castle, an archer shot Richard in the shoulder. The arrow was hacked out, but gangrene set in. Richard realized that he was dying and asked the archer, whose name was Bertram, to come to his deathbed. He pardoned him, gave him 100 shillings and set him free. Then, in agony, he died. Richard the Lionheart, the finest crusader of all time, died at the age of forty-one, without an heir, leaving his neglected throne to his younger brother, John. In his ten-year reign, he had spent only ten months in England. Berengaria, his equally neglected queen, had never even reached England after leaving Acre, and she spent the rest of her life in a French nunnery. As for Bertram the archer, despite the king's pardon, he was flayed alive and hanged.

Perhaps it is fitting that Saladin, Richard's greatest adversary, should have the last word in describing the man renowned in history as Lionheart. Hubert Walter made a pilgrimage to Jerusalem in 1192 and met Saladin there. Discussing Richard, Saladin summed him up in these words:

> I have long since been aware that your king is a man of honor and very brave, but he is imprudent, indeed absurdly so, in the way he plunges in the midst of danger and in his reckless indifference to his own safety. For my own part, however powerful a king I might be, I would like to have wisdom and moderation rather than an excessive boldness.

It was a shrewd judgment.

The Later Crusades and Their Consequences

The Crusades had started in 1095, and Richard died in 1199, more than a hundred years later. In that period of time, Jerusalem had been captured and then lost again. Then, thanks to Richard's negotiations with Saladin, a compromise had been reached whereby Christian pilgrims had free access to the holy places, and European settlers were allowed to remain in the lands won by the crusaders along the coast of Palestine.

This may have been a sensible solution, but it did not satisfy the Christians. For them, the capture of Jerusalem

In many ways the Muslim culture the crusaders set out to displace was more advanced than their own. This is a page from a fourteenth-century Arab mathematical treatise.

itself remained their ultimate dream. Because of this, in the course of the next hundred years, no fewer than five other Crusades were made by various European kings and princes, and almost every one of these met with disaster and failure. There was a brief period of seven years from 1222 to 1229 when, by negotiation, Jerusalem came under Christian rule again, but this agreement quickly broke down.

The most amazing Crusades of all, besides those mounted by kings and princes, were the two Children's Crusades. In 1221, a French shepherd boy named Stephen traveled around France persuading thousands of children to leave home and travel to Jerusalem with him, convinced that God would support them because of their innocence and purity. Sadly, a pair of rogues named Hugh the Iron and William the Pig put them onboard their ships at Marseilles, and the children were sold off into slavery. A similar group set off from Germany led by a boy named Nicholas, and they, too, either died of cold and hunger or were never heard from again.

Eventually, in 1291, after the Eighth Crusade had failed, the great city-fortress of Acre fell to the Muslims, led by Sultan al-Ashraf Khalil. After this, the European settlers pulled out and left Palestine forever. It may appear that the two centuries of crusading effort led to absolutely nothing, and that the whole movement was a sheer waste of time. Nevertheless, there were many benefits as the two civilizations met and intermingled. At that time the Muslim world was much more advanced than the West, and the crusaders experienced much that was new to them.

An Arab physician prepares medicine, from a thirteenth-century Islamic manuscript. Arab doctors came to be respected throughout Europe for their superior knowledge.

In terms of learning, the Europeans gained knowledge about medical treatments and also about astronomy and mathematics. Arabic numerals were introduced to replace the more cumbersome Roman number system. The Europeans adopted Eastern inventions such as ships' rudders and windmills. They learned new techniques in papermaking and glassmaking. They borrowed many innovations in architecture, especially in castle building. They developed a taste for luxuries such as silks, perfumes, carpets, tapestries, brocades, and decorated leatherwork. Even the very ideas of universities and hospitals were adopted from the East.

Obviously, much of this would have arrived in Europe without the Crusades. Nevertheless, the crusading movement helped to speed up the process of cultural contact. Above all, no one will ever forget the crucial role played by Richard I in this dramatic period of history.

Glossary

Adriatic   The part of the Mediterranean Sea that lies between the east coast of Italy and the west coast of Greece.

Anatolia   The part of Turkey that lies in Asia.

Byzantium   Also called Constantinople, and now named Istanbul. The eastern capital of the old Roman Empire.

Crusade   A religious war waged by Christians. It derives from the Latin word *crux*, a "cross," and refers to the cross-shaped piece of cloth that was sewn onto the tunics of the crusading princes and knights.

galley   A long low-built ship with one deck, propelled by oars and sails.

gangrene   Decaying flesh, deadly in the Middle Ages, when there were no antibiotic treatments.

habit   The ankle-length garment worn by monks.

minstrel   A medieval musician either attached to a noble household or else one who traveled from castle to castle, singing and accompanying himself on a stringed instrument.

Moravil   The present-day Czech Republic.

Muslim   A person who believes in the faith of Islam, taught by the prophet Muhammad (c. 570–c. 632).

Navarre   An ancient kingdom in northern Spain. Richard's queen, Berengaria, came from Navarre.

Outremer   A name given to the territory in the Holy Land occupied by the Christians. It is derived from the French and means "beyond the sea."

pilgrim   One who travels to visit a holy place. During the Middle Ages, thousands of people went on pilgrimages, not only to Jerusalem and the Holy Land, but also to the shrines of saints throughout all the Christian countries of Europe.

pope   The head of the Roman Catholic Church, and therefore the leader of Christians throughout the world. In medieval Europe even kings and emperors were considered to be under his rule.

Saracens   The name given by crusaders to their Muslim opponents. As for the Muslims, they called the crusaders "Franks," because so many of them came from France or were of Norman French descent.

Seljuk Turks   A race of nomadic shepherds coming originally from central Asia. They were converted to Islam and were fiercely determined to extend their faith as they spread westward.

trebuchet   A medieval engine of war for launching large stones.

Winchester   An ancient city in southern England, formerly the capital of England. Its cathedral was of special royal importance.

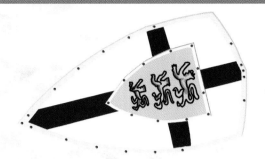

For More Information

The Columbia University Medieval Guild
602 Philosophy Hall
Columbia University
New York, NY 10027
e-mail: cal36@columbia.edu
Web site: http://www.cc.columbia.edu/cu/medieval

The Dante Society of America
Brandeis University
MS 024
P.O. Box 549110
Waltham, MA 02454-9110
e-mail: dsa@dantesociety.org
Web site: http://www.dantesociety.org/index.html

International Courtly Literature Society
North American Branch
c/o Ms. Sara Sturm-Maddox
Department of French and Italian
University of Massachusetts at Amherst
Amherst, MA 01003
e-mail: ssmaddox@frital.umass.edu
Web site: http://www-dept.usm.edu/~engdept/icls/
    iclsnab.htm

Medieval Academy of America
1430 Massachusetts Avenue
Cambridge, MA 02138
(617) 491-1622
e-mail: speculum@medievalacademy.org
Web site: http://www.medievalacademy.org/t_bar_2.htm

Rocky Mountain Medieval and Renaissance Association
Department of English Language and Literature
University of Northern Iowa
Cedar Falls, IA 50614-0502
(319) 273-2089
e-mail: jesse.swan@uni.edu
Web site: http://www.uni.edu/~swan/rmmra/rocky.htm

Web Sites

Due to the changing nature of Internet links, the Rosen
Publishing Group, Inc., has developed an online list of
Web sites related to the subject of this book. This site is
updated regularly. Please use this link to access the list:

http://www.rosenlinks.com/lma/rltc

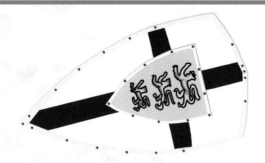

For Further Reading

Clare, John D. *Knights in Armour* (I Was There series). London: The Bodley Head, 1991.

Crisp, Peter. *The Crusades.* London: Wayland Publishers Ltd., 1992.

Gravett, Christopher. *Knight* (Eyewitness Guides). New York: Dorling Kindersley, 1993.

Hodges, Michael. *How It Was: The Crusades*. London: B.T. Batsford Ltd., 1995.

Konstam, Angus. *Historical Atlas of the Crusades*. London: Thalamus Publishing, 2002.

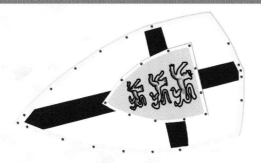

Bibliography

Bridge, Antony. *The Crusades.* London: Granada
    Publishing, 1980.

Esposito, John L., ed. *The Oxford History of Islam.* Oxford,
    England: Oxford University Press, 1999.

Gillingham, John. *The Life and Times of Richard I.*
    London: Weidenfeld and Nicolson, 1973.

Hallam, Elizabeth, ed. *Chronicles of the Crusades.*
    London: Weidenfeld and Nicolson, 1989.

Jones, John. *The Mediaeval World.* Nashville, TN: Thomas
    Nelson & Sons, 1992.

Oldenbourg, Zoé. *The Crusades.* New York: Phoenix
    Press, 2001.

Runciman, Steven. *A History of the Crusades, Vol. II.* New
    York: Cambridge University Press, 1952.

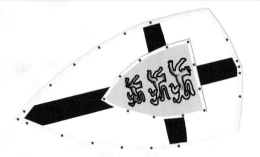

Index

About the Author

David Hilliam was educated at both Oxford and Cambridge Universities and has taught history at schools in Salisbury, Winchester, Canterbury, London, and Versailles. He is passionately interested in the British monarchy. His books include *Kings, Queens, Bones; Bastards, Monarchs, Murders, and Mistresses;* and his latest, *Crown, Orb, and Sceptre,* which is an account of all the British royal coronations. At present he lives and teaches in Dorset, England.

Photo Credits

Cover © Musée Condé Chantilly/The Art Archive; pp. 4, 14, 18, 21, 26, 28, 32, 54 © AKG London; p. 7 © Museo Camillo Leone Vercelli/Dagli Orti/The Art Archive; p. 10 © British Library, London, England; pp. 12, 42 © The Bridgeman Art Library; pp. 15, 40 © Sonia Halliday Photographs and Laura Lushington; pp. 16, 34 © Jane Taylor/Sonia Halliday Photographs; pp. 22–23, 30, 44, 48 © British Library/AKG London; p. 25 © Jean-François Amelot/AKG London; p. 37 © British Museum/The Art Archive; p. 39 © Sonia Halliday Photographs; p. 50 © Erich Lessing/AKG London; p. 52 © Christie's Images Ltd.

Designer: Nelson Sà; **Editor:** Jake Goldberg; **Photo Researcher:** Elizabeth Loving